A Year of Magick

Ashleigh Long

 BookLeaf Publishing

Presentation by *BookLeaf Publishing*

Web: www.bookleafpub.com

E-mail: info@bookleafpub.com

ISBN: 9789357740104

First edition 2023

These words are dedicated to the broom closet.

ACKNOWLEDGEMENT

Thank you Dan, for being my confidant throughout this process.

New Moon

Pause.
Take a moment.
Reflect on who you are.
Realise where you are.
Just because the sky seems dark
Doesn't mean she left us alone.
She is only resting a moment,
Letting us find our guiding stars.
Decide on which path is yours
Throughout the next cycle,
And consider each step
That will get you there.
Now is not a time for action
But soon it will be,
And when that time comes
We will be prepared;
But just for now,
Enjoy where you are.
Take a moment.
Pause.

Yule

The day is short;
The dark lasts so long;
We light our hearths
To keep us strong.
Time to let go
Of what does not serve us,
So we can advance
With renewed purpose.
We'll feast upon
The years harvest,
When summers heat
Seems its farthest.
As the sun climbs
It's warmth is felt:
The land will soften,
The ice will melt.
Buds and beasts
Will re-emerge.
To the joys of life
All will serge.

Water

I enter the deep blue and look forward;
Clearly see what is and what will be.
The undulating tide washes away the dirt and
hurt;
With ebb and flow the feeling swells.
I am cleansed.
I am healed.
I am free.

Move through the vast expanse ever onward,
Knowing where I am and where I've been.
The ever changing terrain brings realization
Of the depths of our internal wells.
I feel connected.
I feel protected.
I feel like me.

Imbolc

Time to welcome in the spring,
For sun to shine and flowers to bloom;
Excited for what will begin
Now the seasons change and it's getting warm.
Welcome back the warmth and light;
The days grow longer all the time.
The buds are such a welcome sight,
And creatures emerge from winter slumber.
We each arise from our winter nest,
And prepare to plant what we later harvest.
Remember now that we are blessed,
As all the gods share nature's bounty.

Cauldron

Holding onto secrets
And guarding wishes,
Stands the most magical
Of household dishes!
With round pot-belly
And three stout legs,
Filled right to the brim
Or with nothing but dregs.
Gaze deep down,
Into my dark heart;
Let fates curtains
Begin to part.
Now give into it,
The vast sensation,
Knowing inside ourselves
We hold creation.

Waxing Moon

She swells. She grows.
She expands and flows;
Encouraging the growth
And the progress.
With each step forward
Well laid plans start taking form.
As she rounds she brings
Brightness to our lives.
Don't stop moving ever forwards,
There will be time to rest soon;
Right now we take action,
Bring forth our needs and desires,
And all of her encouragement
Assists with this journey;
But you know in your heart
This path is your own,
And if you stop walking
She will not force you.
So take her encouragement
And take her guidance,
Expanding and growing
Into who you wish to be.

Ostara

Night and day in perfect balance;
Let's welcome new life.
A time to start fresh once again,
And put aside past strife.

After winters rest the time has come
To work and toil;
Time to dig and plough the land,
And seed the soil.

Fertile lands and creature swell,
With abundance they're blessed.
Watch each bird return back to the land
To build their nest.

Ask now for nature's warmth and care
For a harvest that's plentiful.
Celebrate the joys of life and renewal
Join in our festival!

Air

Often heard, always felt,
But never seen or held.
Ever present necessity of all life created.
Constantly moving, ever changing.
Carrying song and fragrance,
Roaming free across land and sea,
Fetching inspiration from far and wide.
Breathe deeply and take it all in.
Watch closely for the path
That each wind takes:
They are carving the way
For what is to come.

Beltane

The warm sun coming fast.
The warm fire aglow.
The warm embrace we share.

We'll dance through the night
    Until the small hours,
Twisting our crowns
    From petals and leaves.

Let the flames guide us.
Let the smoke cleanse us.
Let the ashes bless us.

We'll dance for our queen,
    Dressed all up in flowers;
Twisting our ribbons
    Into delicate weaves.

Broom

Sweep away the dust and dirt;
Sweep away the pain and hurt;
Sweep away all fight and fear;
Sweep away all bad from here;
Sweep until the dark has gone;
Sweep until the light has come;
Sweep until all looks its best;
Sweep until all spirits rest.

Full Moon

Her light washes over all
We have built this season in life;
Let us honour our accomplishments
In her shining presence.

She fills all with her power,
Rinsing all free of stagnation;
Cleanse away the negative
With her whisper-like touch.

Her gentle embrace heals us
From deep within our souls;
Let mind and body rejuvenate
Thanks to her shared power.

We each stare at the sky
Taking in her beauty and grace,
But now let us give thanks
For each gift she brings.

Litha

Bright sun lasts all through,
The longest day stretches on.
Out in the light is the best way
To enjoy that summer has come.
The crops grow strong and tall
Ready for the harvest;
Thank and encourage the earth
As she prepares her best.
Flower out in full bloom
Bring joy to each life,
Embrace each second
As we all thrive.
The wheel will turn again,
For now enjoy each moment.
This long day of light
Is nature's present.

Fire

Destroying and burning
And taking all;
Creating and changing
In the space left behind.
Such a great power
Must be carefully controlled,
Or the heat of passion
Will leave us nothing.
Protecting and serving,
Through making or taking;
It may strengthen
Or it may weaken,
But it will shine bright
From within us all.

Lughasadh

The fields have started to ripen;
Let us start bringing in our crop.
As we harvest the first grain
Know a blessed event has arrived.
Time to begin the harvest;
We'll feast upon our bounty
And give thanks back to the earth.
Let's reap what we have sown
And begin to bake our loaves.
This is only the first taste,
There is much more to arrive
If our lands have been blessed.
Show gratitude for what you have,
And even more for what's to come.

Candle

Tell me what you desire.
Bathe and bless me,
Carve in your hopes.

Send off your wish with touch of fire.
Hold me with care,
Speak your need.

Worship at my small pyre.
Revere my light,
Hold your want close.

Eventually I will expire.
Watch my smoke,
It speaks your prayer.

The vapours rise ever higher.
My work is done,
Your will is heard.

Wanning Moon

She thins and shrinks,
Reminds us to let go,
To cast aside that which holds us back.
Your net was cast wide,
Now you must focus in.
Rejuvenate. Regenerate.
As her light decreases, remember your goals.
Reflect on your path,
Where it has taken you;
Do not stop yet,
These last few step can make the difference
Between reaching the end,
And missing the mark;
And if you release what weighs you down,
You'll get even further,
Closer to your end goal.

Mabon

The fields have started to ripen;
Let us start bringing in our crop.
As we harvest the first grain
Know a blessed event has arrived.
Time to begin the harvest;
We'll feast upon our bounty
And give thanks back to the earth.
Let's reap what we have sown
And begin to bake our loaves.
This is only the first taste,
There is much more to arrive
If our lands have been blessed.
Show gratitude for what you have,
And even more for what's to come.

Earth

Still and grounded,
Deep and quiet,
Holding the seeds of all.
Shaped and formed
Into each part of life,
Nourishing all
And sheltering all
That springs forth.
Fertile and vast,
Ever moulding to change,
But constantly present.
Each tree that reaches up,
Each creature the crawls ahead,
Can also reach down
And thank the earth
That lies beneath them.

Samhain

The last harvest is in and the winter begins;
Let's feast by the fire before darkness returns.
Enjoy the colourful sights on display
As trees change leaves through orange and red.
Those departed once again return,
Welcome in your kin with fine gifts
Of food and drink and love aplenty.
When the deceased have taken their fill
Share hearth and home with those most in need.
Be careful should you walk the roads,
Dark spirits also surround us;
So hide your face behind a mask
Lest you be carried away to their realms.
If you dare look ahead to futures reflection
Now is the time to take in the sight;
But be wary now, for what you see
May come to haunt you.

Crystal

Gaze deep.
Find each minute imperfection;
See the light shift as each stone demands.
Colours dance,
Bringing visions of things that will be;
As you star now you are certain
This energy runs through all.

Hold tight.
Your touch will affect your perception;
Feel the power of the earth in your hands.
Held in a trance,
Bringing feelings of peace and of glee;
With the contact lifts a great burden
And begins the pull to a great call.

Witch

You say it like its a bad thing;
A sad thing;
A fad thing.
I feel so very rejected;
So very neglected;
So very dissected.
I won't be denied anymore;
Hide anymore;
Stand aside anymore.
My faith is the cycle of life.
My temple is the Earth.
My message is joy and hope.

With these word I say my prayer;
I cast my spell;
My heart wants to share;
My soul starts to yell:

About my great glad thing,
That I can be fully accepted,
And hold my head up with pride evermore.

www.ingramcontent.com/pod-product-compliance
Lightning Source LLC
Chambersburg PA
CBHW071719160726

R18582000001B/R185820PG48003CBX00001B/1